CAREER PUPPETS
by
Dwayne Douglas Kohn

Smart As A Fox Teaching Materials are available from your local teacher supply store or purchase online at: www.MisterKindergarten.com. For materials in Spanish, please visit: www.PrimerGrado.com. We publish over 200 titles in a variety of languages.

SMART AS A FOX
BOX 4334
OCEANSIDE, CALIFORNIA
92052-4334

MW01292245

CAREER PUPPETS

With these easy-to-make patterns, your students will be able to make 20 paper bag puppets for the career of their choice!

You can print out a color copy and laminate it for a teacher sample or for use year after year in a Career play center.

MAKING PUPPETS

1. Color in both parts of the puppet (head and body) using crayons, colored pencils, watercolor paints, etc.

2. Carefully cut out the two parts of the puppet on the solid outline.

3. Glue the head of the puppet onto the bottom flap of a paper lunch bag.

4. Glue the body of the puppet on the bag with the inside of the mouth under the flap. The tongue should be visible only when the mouth is open.

5. You may also wish to cut out the name of the career and glue it to front or back of the puppet.

6. Customize your puppet by adding glitter, buttons, yarn, cotton balls, etc.

WRITING

We have included special stationery to fit on the back of each paper bag puppet. There are two sheets on the page. Simply cut them out and glue to the back of the bags. Have students practice writing that puppet's name ("police," "doctor," etc.), simple sentences about the career depicted ("I want to be a teacher."), or an entire story about their puppet.

CAREER PUPPETS

The following are the puppets included in this title (male and female version of each):

Athlete, Cook/Chef, Doctor, Firefighter, Mechanic, Painter/Artist, Police Officer, Salesperson, Scientist, Teacher.

Note that many of the puppets can easily be used for numerous careers. For example, the mechanic could be a plumber, the salesperson could be an author, the teacher could be a businessperson, etc.

CLASSROOM USE

Have the students cut out and glue the description of the career to the back of the puppet and then read it aloud to the class as part of their presentation.

Look for our complete series of paper bag puppets: ABC Puppets, Career Puppets, Wild Animal Puppets and more!

Smart As a Fox Teaching Materials publishes over 200 titles geared to the primary classroom in a variety of languages.

Look for us online at:

www.MrKindergarten.com
or
www.PrimerGrado.com
(Spanish)
or
www.SpeakChineseToday.com
(Chinese)

ATHLETE

Imagine getting paid for playing ball! It can happen if you are very good at the sport you play. But it isn't as easy as it seems. You must be one of the very best players in the entire country to be able to make a living as an athlete. It takes years of hard training and effort. Even then you might not make the team. To be on the safe side, most athletes stay in school to learn. This way if they can't get a job as an athlete, at least they will be able to find another type of job. Remember, most of those who do make it to the "big leagues" only last a few years.

Cut out and glue to the back of your puppet.

COOK

I love food. How about you? If you do then you might want to become a chef or cook. We work in restaurants preparing the meals. To be a good cook you will need to be able to read the recipes and know how to correctly measure the ingredients. You will learn how to chop vegetables and add the right amount of spices to create wonderful masterpieces! You might work in a small cafe or a famous restaurant in a big city. Either way you'll be happy knowing that people love the food you make for them!

www.MisterKindergarten.com

Athlete

www.MisterKindergarten.com

Athlete

www.MisterKindergarten.com

Chef

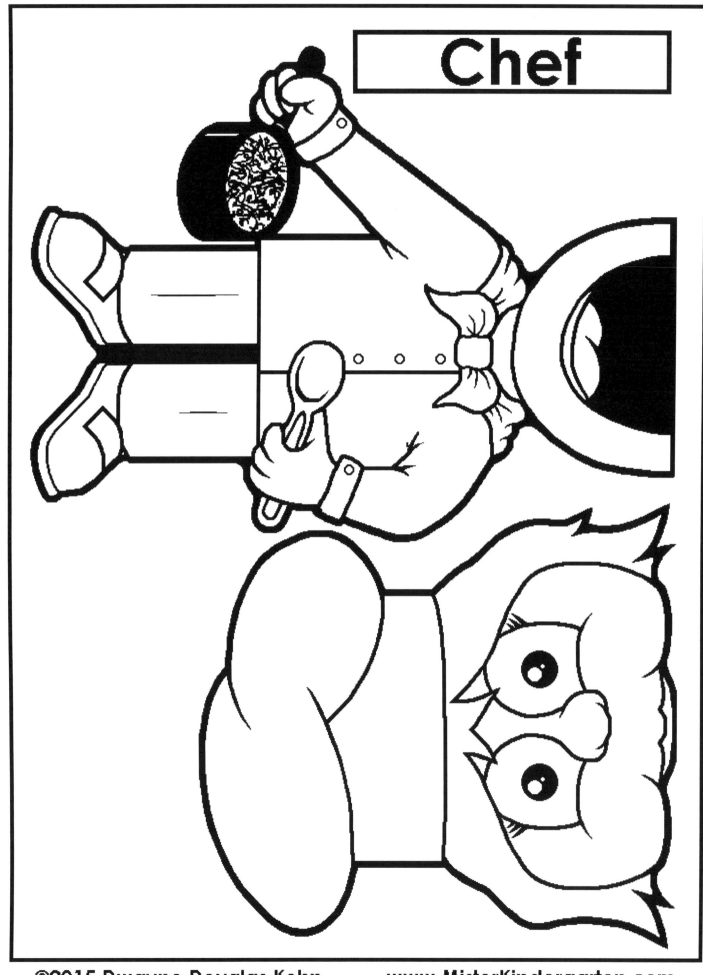

Cook

DOCTOR

Do you like to help people? You might wish to become a doctor. It takes many years of study to be a physician and there are many kinds of doctors. Doctors tell you why you feel sick and give you medicine to make you feel better. A podiatrist specializes in feet. Ophthalmologists concentrate on eyes. Some doctors treat your skin. Others take care of your heart. Radiologists take pictures, called x-rays, that can see inside of your body. Another type of doctor is a surgeon. Surgeons operate on your body when something is wrong. Many doctors study and try to find cures for diseases so that we may all live longer, healthier lives.

Cut out and glue to the back of your puppet.

FIREFIGHTER

Would you like to be a firefighter? It can be a very dangerous job. They risk their lives almost every day trying to save lives and property. Sometimes they must enter a burning building in order to rescue people trapped inside. When the doors are locked, they use an axe to break them down. While at the fire station, they must be ready, day or night, for any kind of emergency. Firefighters also teach people how to make their homes safer. Make sure that you have smoke detectors in your house and that you know what to do in case of a fire. If you see a fire, call the firefighters by dialing 9-1-1.

©2015 Dwayne Douglas Kohn   www.MisterKindergarten.com

Doctor

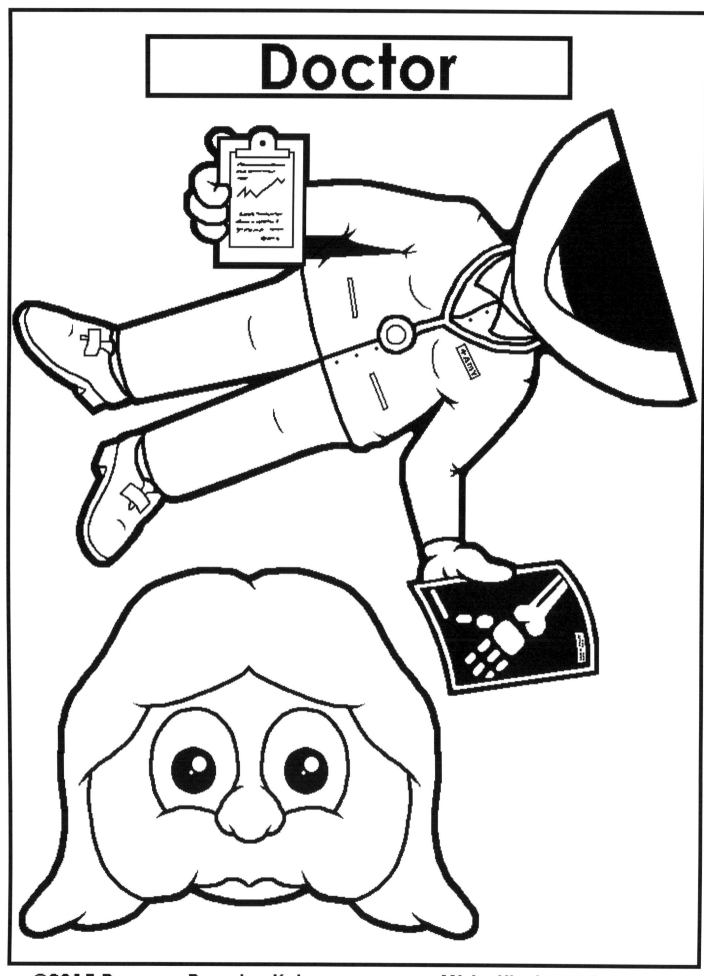

Doctor

www.MisterKindergarten.com

Firefighter

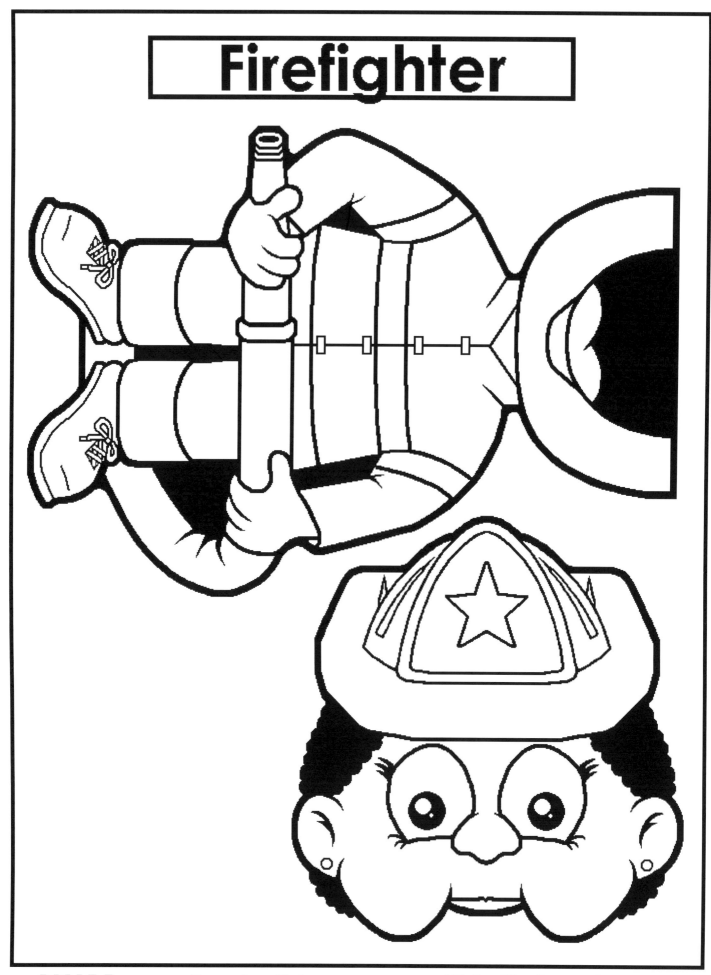

www.MisterKindergarten.com

Firefighter

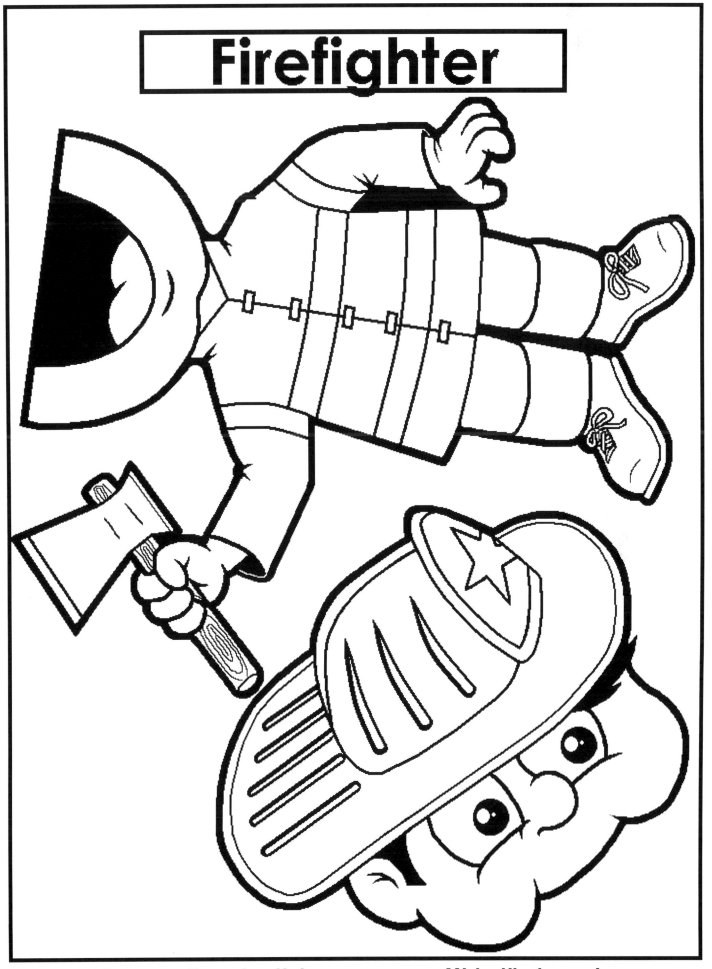

MECHANIC

Do you like to take things apart and put them back together again? Do you wonder how machines work? Are you able to fix things when they break? If so, you might want to be a mechanic! Some mechanics fix cars. Others work on television sets and computers. To be a good mechanic you need to learn all that you can about machines, electricity and tools. You need to be able to read the manuals that tell you what the different parts are for and how they go together. You must also be very patient. Finding out what is wrong and how to fix it can take a long time!

Cut out and glue to the back of your puppet.

PAINTER

Do you love to create beautiful things? You would do well with a job in the arts! You could be an artist and draw or paint for a living. Or maybe a sculptor and make a wonderful statue to put in the center of your local park. Do you like to draw houses? You could become a world-reknown architect and create the mansions of the rich and famous. You might be a fashion clothing designer and invent the next new "look." Maybe a cartoonist or animator is what you want to be when you grow up. Whether you paint pictures or paint houses, you will make the world a more beautiful place.

©2015 Dwayne Douglas Kohn   www.MisterKindergarten.com

Mechanic

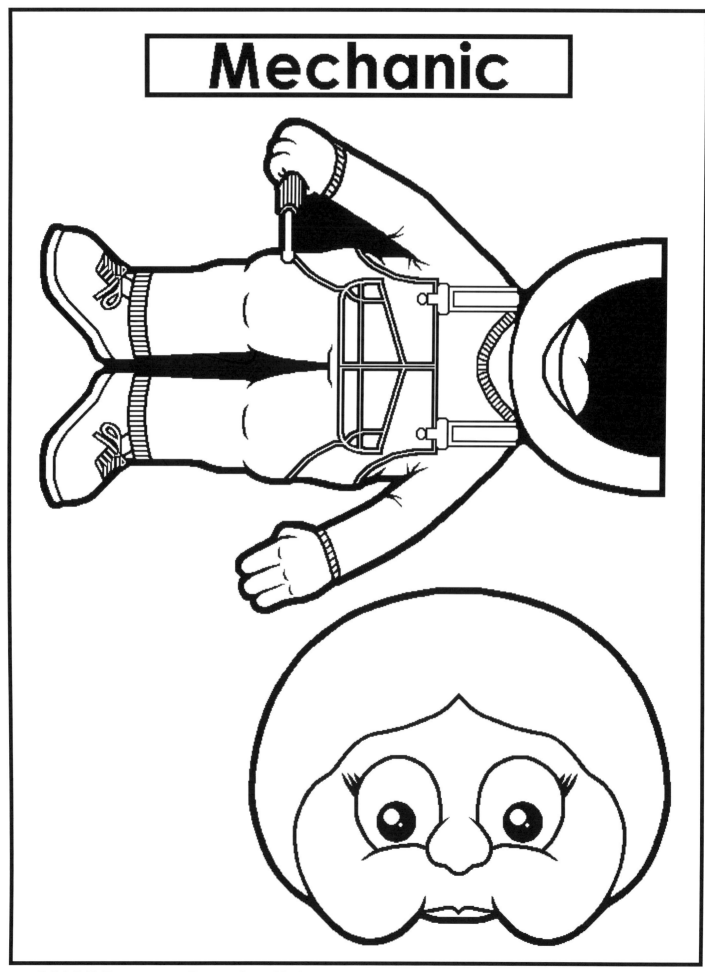

Mechanic

Painter

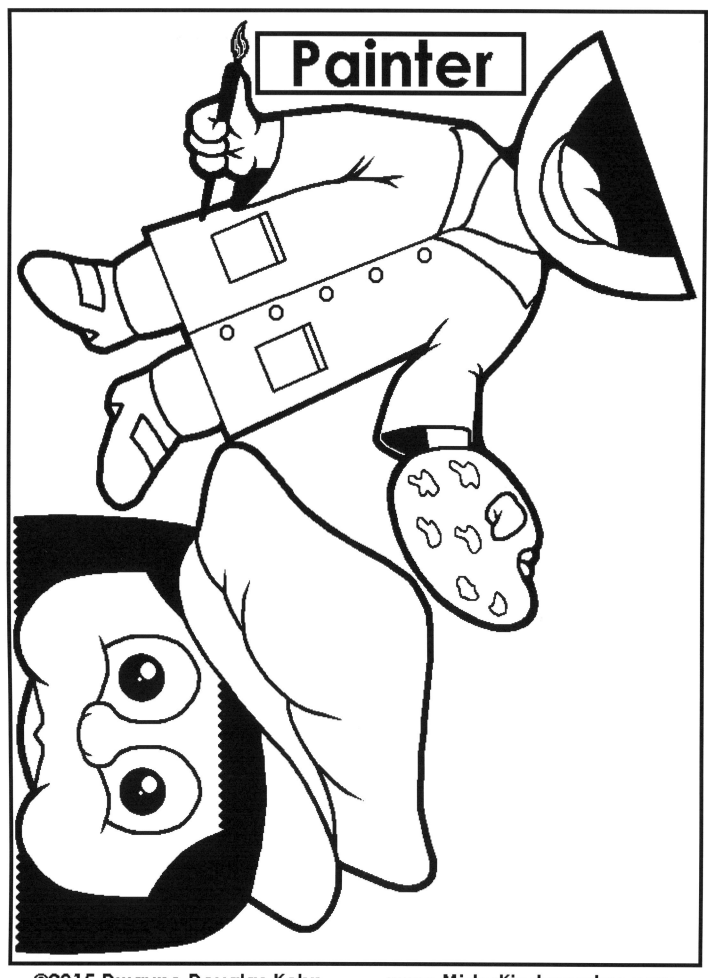

www.MisterKindergarten.com

Painter

www.MisterKindergarten.com

POLICE OFFICER

Have you ever wondered what it might be like to be a police officer? It isn't always like you see on television. There are many kinds of police officers. Not all of them chase bad guys! Some are traffic cops. They make sure that people obey the laws while driving. In some big cities, police officers help to direct traffic. Some officers are called detectives and don't even wear a uniform. They look for clues to help solve a case. Other officers patrol on foot, in a police car, on a motorcycle or even on horseback or bicycle. But they all are here to help and protect us.

Cut out and glue to the back of your puppet.

SALESPERSON

Do you like to talk to people? Have others told you that you have a great personality? Have you might have what it takes to be a salesperson! You might have a job in a big department store or sell for an international company. You might travel across the country, or even around the world, trying to sell things to people or companies. You will need to be able to read and write very well in order to sell your product and sign the contracts. You will use your math skills when you add up the prices of all of the products you sell!

www.MisterKindergarten.com

Police Officer

 www.MisterKindergarten.com

Police Officer

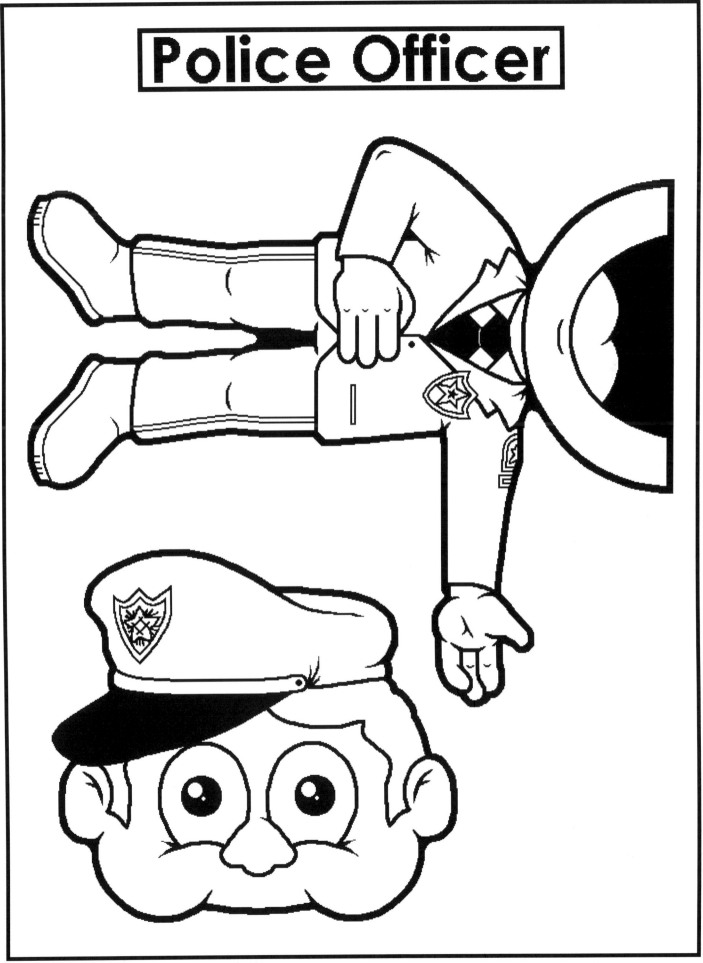

www.MisterKindergarten.com

Salesperson

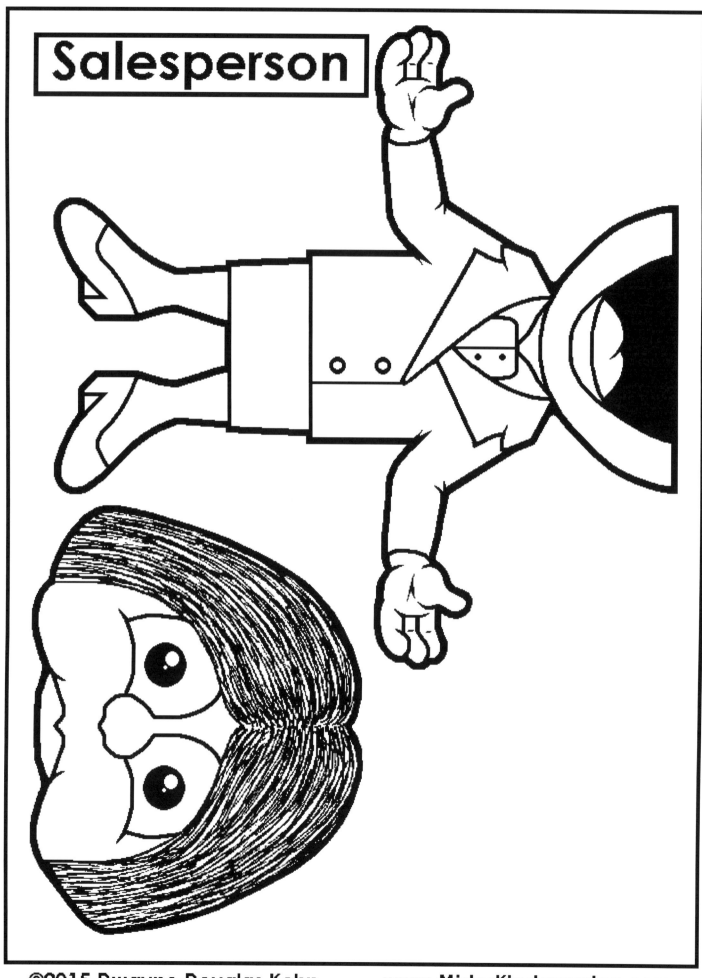

Salesperson

www.MisterKindergarten.com

SCIENTIST

If you like to experiment with things, then I have the job for you! You can be a scientist and try to make the world a better place. Scientists are always trying to figure out how things work and to better understand them. They attempt to find cures to diseases or invent things to make our lives more enjoyable. You will need to know a lot of science and math. You will also need to do a lot of research. Scientists may have many failures before they are finally successful. Their work saves many, many lives around the world. Maybe you will be the one who discovers a cure for cancer, diabetes, or any of the many other horrible deseases that exist.

Cut out and glue to the back of your puppet.

TEACHER

Do you enjoy working with children? Then maybe being a teacher is the job for you! To be a good teacher you need to know a lot of information and be able to present it in a way that keeps the class interested. You need to know about history, art and science. You need to be able to explain how to add, subtract, multiply and divide. As a teacher, you will teach your students how to read and write. As you can see, one needs to study hard to become a teacher. After all, how can you teach your students something if you don't know it first?

     www.MisterKindergarten.com

Scientist

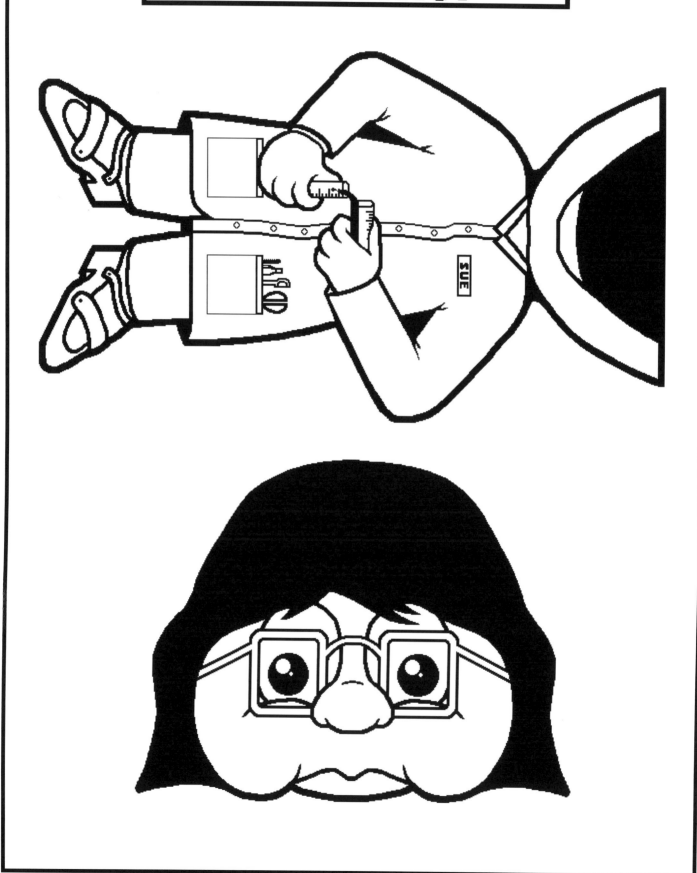

www.MisterKindergarten.com

Scientist

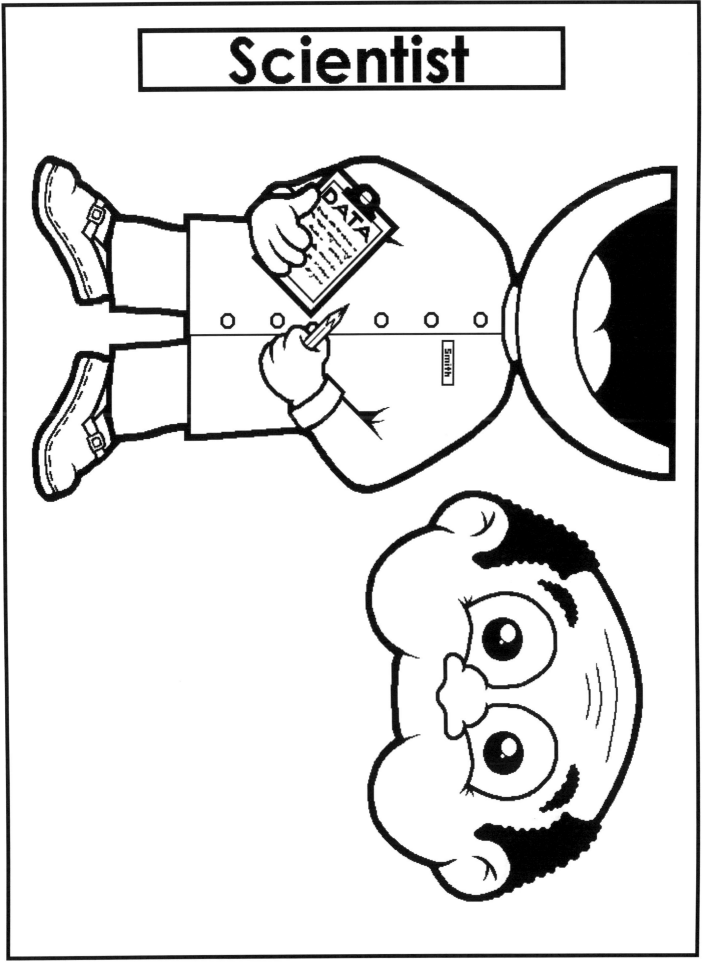

www.MisterKindergarten.com

Teacher

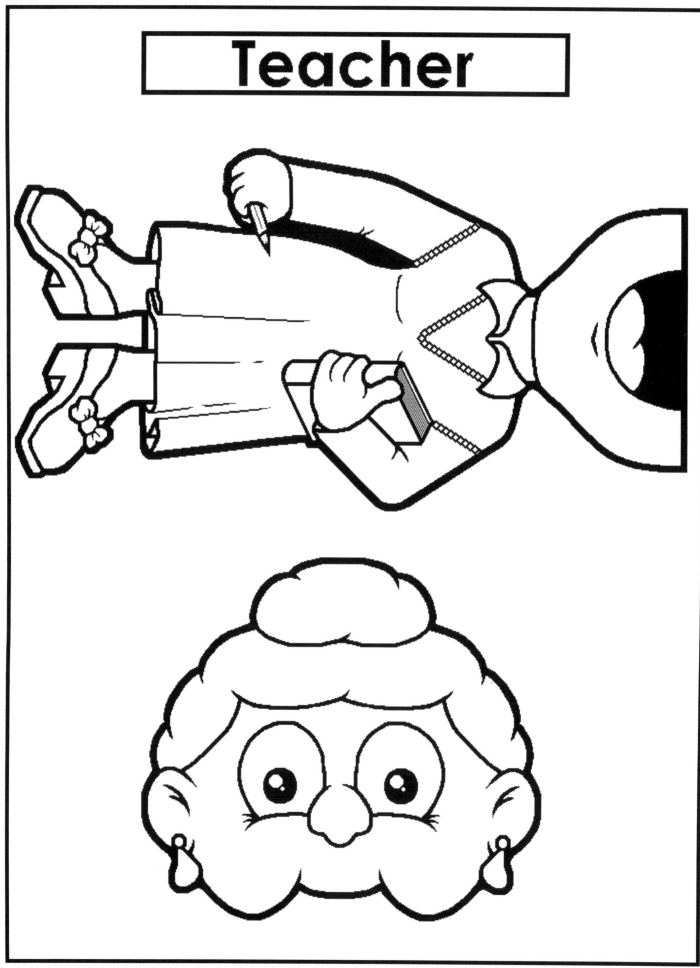

www.MisterKindergarten.com

Teacher

Name:

Cut out and glue to the back of your puppet.

Name:

Made in the USA
Middletown, DE
16 June 2017